Common Core L
Environme

By C;

Published by Gallopade International, Inc.
©Carole Marsh/Gallopade
Printed in the U.S.A. (Peachtree City, Georgia)

TABLE OF CONTENTS

G: Includes Graphic Organizer

GO: Graphic Organizer is also available 8½" x 11" online
download at www.gallopade.com/client/go
(numbers above correspond to the graphic organizer numbers online)

What Is Environmental Science?

Read the text and answer the questions.

Just as it is important to clean up and take care of the house you live in, it is equally important to care for Earth. After all, it is where we all live! Taking care of the environment is so important that there is a whole field of science dedicated to it called Environmental Science.

The purpose of Environmental Science is to explore and explain the interaction between humans and Earth. Environmental scientists study how life on Earth endures, how humans interact with Earth, what causes environmental problems, and how these problems can be solved. In other words, Environmental Science studies how human actions impact the planet.

Humans have been concerned with protecting their environment since ancient times. History tells us of people moving to new land once pasturelands became barren and overused soil became useless for farming. When industries grew in the 18th and 19th centuries, polluted air and water from factories and large populations became a concern.

Studying Environmental Science helps scientists come up with solutions to issues like climate change, animal extinction, and pollution. But scientists are not the only ones who can help save Earth. We can all do our part every day to protect our planet!

1. Summarize the main idea of the text.

2. Use a dictionary to define interaction and endures as they are used in the text.

3. Why is the study of Environmental Science important? Cite evidence from the text for your answer.

4. Work in groups. Make a display on posterboard using photographs and text to show examples of environmental issues present in our world today. Discuss your posters as a class.

Environmental Science Vocabulary

Use a dictionary and other resources to complete the graphic organizer for each vocabulary word.

atmosphere   environment   hydrosphere

biosphere   extinction   interact

ecology   fossil fuel   population

ecosystem   geosphere   recycle

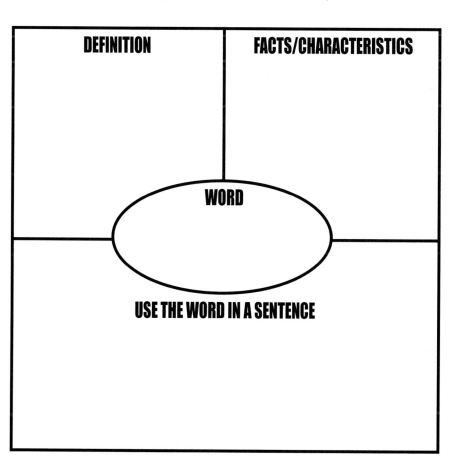

Earth's Systems

Use online or classroom resources to complete the graphic organizer. Define and describe Earth's four major systems.

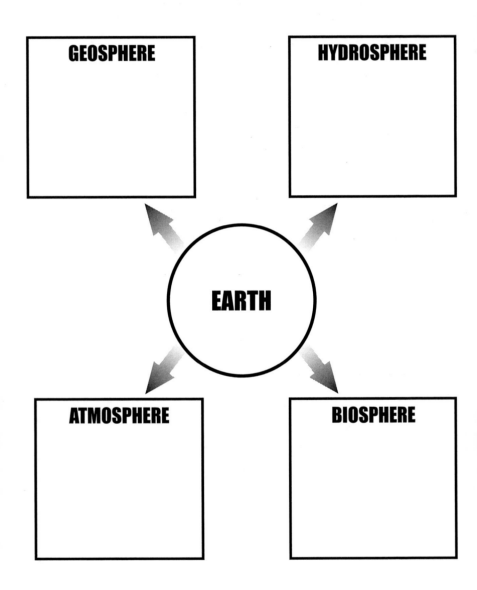

GEOSPHERE

HYDROSPHERE

EARTH

ATMOSPHERE

BIOSPHERE

The Water Cycle

Read the text and answer the questions.

The water cycle is the most powerful force at work on our planet. Each day, energy from the sun evaporates a trillion tons of water from Earth's surface into the atmosphere. And each day, much of that water returns to Earth in the form of rain, sleet, snow, or hail.

The water cycle has four main processes: *evaporation, condensation, precipitation,* and *accumulation. Evaporation* occurs when the sun warms the water in rivers, lakes, and oceans, and turns it a gas (water vapor). The water vapor rises into the atmosphere. *Condensation* occurs when the vapor cools and changes into a liquid, forming clouds.

When the clouds become too heavy with condensed water, they release some of that water in the form of rain, hail, sleet, or snow. This process is known as <u>precipitation</u>. Rain and other forms of precipitation fall back to Earth where they <u>accumulate</u> in oceans, lakes, rivers, and pockets underground. Then, the water cycle starts all over again!

1. A. Use a dictionary to write the two meanings of <u>precipitation</u>.
   B. Use a dictionary to define <u>accumulate</u> as it is used in the text.

2. Use the text to label each process of the water cycle in the diagram.
   A. evaporation B. condensation C. precipitation D. accumulation

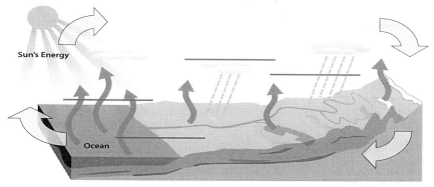

Sun's Energy

Ocean

3. Identify which part of the water cycle each word belongs to.
   A. clouds _____   B. lake _____
   C. water vapor _____   D. snow _____

How Weather Affects Landforms

Read the text and answer the questions.

Weather has a major effect on Earth's landforms. Over time, landforms can be changed or even destroyed by processes known as *weathering* and *erosion*.

Weathering is the process of breaking down rocks into smaller pieces, such as pebbles, sand, or dirt. There are two types of weathering: *chemical weathering* and *mechanical weathering*. *Chemical weathering* occurs when rock material reacts with a chemical like water, oxygen, or carbon, and changes into a different substance. *Mechanical weathering* occurs when rocks are broken down through physical forces. This weathering could be caused by temperature change, a storm, or people breaking up rocks.

After rocks have been broken down by weathering, the pieces may be moved by wind, water, or ice from one location to another. This is known as *erosion*. Moving water, like rain, waves, or rushing streams and rivers, is a major cause of erosion.

The processes of weathering and erosion take time to change a landscape, but they are powerful forces. No rock is strong enough to withstand them!

1. Fill in the graphic organizer to describe the two types of weathering. Use online resources to list examples of each type.

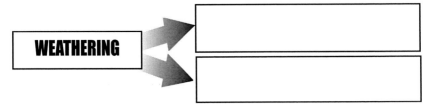

WEATHERING

2. Infer what force caused the erosion displayed by the Grand Canyon in the photograph.

Acid Rain

Read the text and answer the questions.

Water is important for all living creatures. Rain is a source of drinking water for animals and humans, and helps plants and crops grow. However, because of air pollution, rainwater can become dangerous and turn into a hazard known as acid rain.

Acid rain is rainfall made so acidic by pollution that it causes harm to the environment. When fossil fuels like coal, natural gas, and oil are burned by factories, automobiles, or power plants, the gases emitted are released into the atmosphere. Winds may spread the gases for hundreds of miles. The chemicals in these gases mix with the clouds, causing rain, snow, or hail to become very acidic.

Acid raid can have terrible effects on forests, lakes, buildings, and animals. Acid rain strips important minerals from leaves and soil, causing trees and other plants to not grow properly. Without minerals, plants become very weak and can even die. Acidic rainwater collects in lakes, rivers, and streams. If the water becomes too acidic, fish and plants are unable to survive in the environment. Acid rain can destroy buildings by eating away at the metal or stone.

Rain is important for everything living on earth, so it is essential to protect rain by eliminating pollution in the air.

1. Summarize the main idea of the text..

2. Use logical reasoning to number the events in chronological order.
   ____ Rain falls.
   ____ Factory releases chemicals into the air.
   ____ Acidic rain flows into rivers and lakes.
   ____ Wind carries chemicals for many miles.
   ____ Fish and aquatic organisms die.

3. Use the text to list causes and effects of acid rain.

Causes of Acid Rain	Effects of Acid Rain

DATA ANALYSIS

Population and Deforestation

Read the text and analyze the chart.

> Trees are very important to life on Earth. Trees provide homes for many animals and plants. They create oxygen for humans and animals to breathe. They are also the source of many products and medicines.
>
> Deforestation is the removal of the trees in a forest. Trees are cut down to make room for farms, businesses, and homes. They are also cut down for timber and paper products. As the population of Earth increases, so does deforestation.

Population Growth & Forest Loss Since 1990

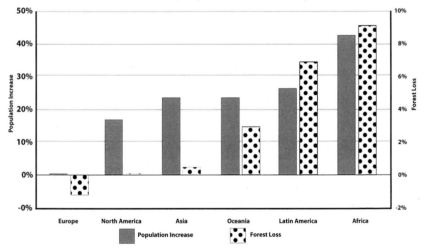

1. A. Which continent showed the most forest loss?
   B. Which continent showed the most population growth?

2. Which continent showed the least forest loss?

3. What does the chart show and the text say about the relationship between population growth and forest loss?

4. Research what countries can do to decrease forest loss even with an increasing population. Write your recommendations in a short essay. Proofread and edit your work. Discuss solutions as a class.

Three Gorges Dam

When humans modify the environment, both positive and negative results can occur. The Three Gorges Dam in China is a good example. The three main purposes for building the dam were improved navigation for ships along the Yangtze River, increased generation of electricity for the huge Chinese population, and better flood control. However, the dam's construction has had some serious negative consequences.

Use online research to find three negative consequences of the Three Gorges Dam. Then use the text and your research to complete the graphic organizer.

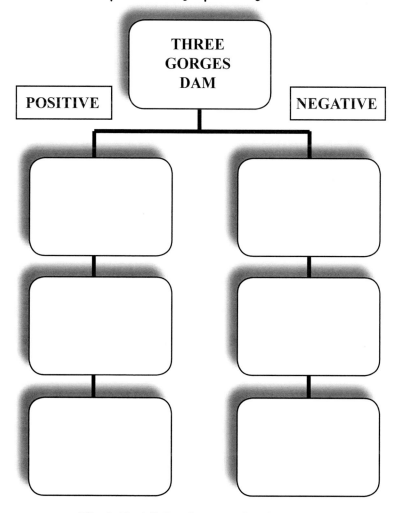

Water on Earth

Use the text and chart to answer the questions.

> Earth is often referred to as the "Blue Planet." About 71% of Earth's surface is covered with water. There is water in the air and clouds, and even under the ground.
>
> Water on Earth is either freshwater or saltwater. Saltwater is found in oceans and makes up 97% of the water on Earth. Because of the salt in saltwater, humans cannot drink it.
>
> Freshwater is water that does not contain a large amount of salt or minerals and can be used by humans. Although all freshwater can be used by humans, not all freshwater can be accessed.
>
> Freshwater is found in three forms on Earth: glaciers, groundwater, and surface water. A *glacier* is a slow-moving mass of ice. Glaciers cover 10 percent of the world's landmass. Glaciers typically remain frozen, even in the summertime. *Groundwater* is water that is found beneath Earth's surface. This water accumulates under the ground from rain, melted snow, and other water that seeps through soil or sand. *Surface water* is any water found on Earth's surface. This can be saltwater found in oceans, or freshwater found in rivers, lakes, streams, and reservoirs.
>
> Although Earth has plenty of water, humans can use less than one percent of it!

1. Use a dictionary to define accessed and reservoirs as they are used in the text. List a synonym for each word.

2. Name the two types of water found on Earth. Which one is most abundant?

3. Create a chart with photographs and descriptions of the three forms of freshwater. Infer which form people can access most easily.

4. Find a photograph of Earth taken from space. Infer why Earth is often referred to as the "Blue Planet."

5. Using the photo, write a narrative from the perspective of an astronaut out in space looking back at Earth. What does he or she see? How does he or she feel looking at the planet from space?

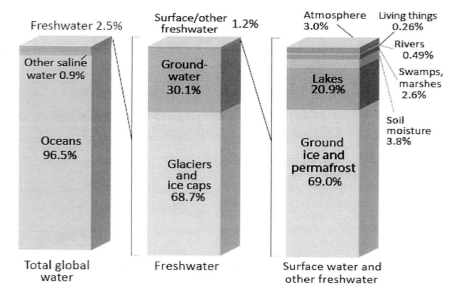

6. Summarize the purpose of each bar chart.

7. A. What is the relationship between the left bar chart and the middle bar chart?
   B. What is the relationship between the middle bar chart and the right bar chart?

8. Analyze percentages in the chart to number freshwater categories from largest (1) to smallest (4).
   _____ Lakes
   _____ Glaciers
   _____ Groundwater
   _____ Rivers

9. Although rivers comprise a small percentage of freshwater on Earth, they provide humans with much of their water. Research where your community gets its water. Predict what would happen if your community's water source became polluted.

10. Use the Venn Diagram to compare saltwater and freshwater.

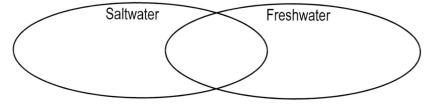

Careers Related to Environmental Science

There are many STEM careers related to the study of Environmental Science. Just a few are listed here. Research each career and write a short job description in the box. Draw a symbol to represent that career.

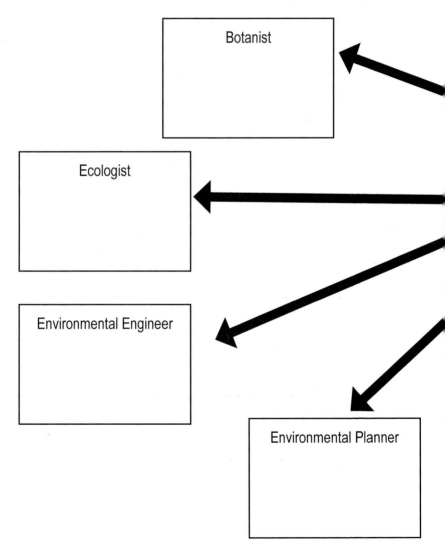

Botanist

Ecologist

Environmental Engineer

Environmental Planner

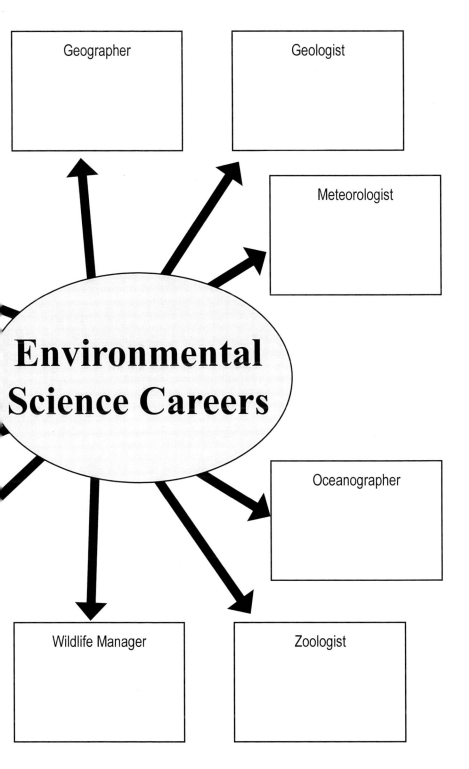

Geographer

Geologist

Meteorologist

Environmental Science Careers

Oceanographer

Wildlife Manager

Zoologist

Bhopal Gas Disaster

Read the text and quotes, and answer the questions.

On December 2-3, 1984, the world's worst industrial disaster occurred at a Union Carbide <u>pesticide</u> plant in Bhopal, Madhya Pradesh, India. An accident allowed toxic gas to be released into the atmosphere. The effects of the accident were devastating. The toxic cloud spread throughout the city, exposing over half a million people to the chemicals. Over time, more than 10,000 people died from the effects of the gas leak. Even today, thousands suffer from <u>chronic illness</u> from being exposed to the gas.

Aziza Sultan, a Bhopal resident, remembers the following:

"At about 12.30 am I woke to the sound of Ruby coughing badly. The room was not dark, there was a street light nearby. In the half light I saw that the room was filled with a white cloud. I heard a great noise of people shouting. They were yelling 'bhaago, bhaago' (run, run). Mohsin started coughing too and then I started coughing with each breath seeming as if we were breathing in fire ..."

Harish Singh Yadav recalls the events that occurred that night:

"We were sleeping, when suddenly my daughter woke us up. She said her eyes were burning. Soon, all of us in the family had the same sensation, as if someone was burning chilies. We all began coughing. Then, when I opened the window, I saw people running for their lives."

1. A. Use a dictionary to define <u>pesticide</u>. List a synonym.
   B. Use a dictionary to define <u>chronic illness</u>. Describe the lasting effects that an industrial disaster can have on a population. Use the text for evidence.

2. Describe the similarities between the two eyewitness accounts.

3. Write a newspaper article describing the Bhopal gas disaster. Use information and quotes from the text, plus additional research. Proofread and edit your work.

4. How does this event show the importance of strict safety rules for factories? Discuss as a class.

CAUSE AND EFFECT
How Animals Become Extinct

Read the text and answer the questions.

What is your favorite animal? Maybe it's an elephant, tiger, gorilla, or panda. Did you know all of these animals are considered to be *endangered*? An animal is endangered when there are very few of them left on Earth, and the species is in danger of dying out. When a species no longer exists, it is considered *extinct*.

Extinction through natural forces usually happens over a long period of time. Animals may become extinct through climate changes, reduced food supply, competition from other species, or a combination of these factors.

Humans are actually the biggest threats to animals. Human interference has increased the rate at which animals become extinct. Several species have been hunted to extinction. Many times, these animals are hunted for their feathers, fur, horns, or other body parts that are considered prizes.

Another contributor to animal extinction is loss of habitat. As trees are cut down and land is developed for human use, an animal's natural habitat is destroyed. Pollution can cause extinction by making an environment unlivable for the animal species.

1. Explain the difference between *endangered* and *extinct*.

2. Research an endangered animal. Write a blog entry about why the animal is endangered and what is being done to help save it.

3. Complete the graphic organizer.

Cause	Effect	Result on Animal Species
Climate changes over period of time		
Trees cut down for human use		
Humans hunting endangered species		
Pollution of the environment		

People and the Environment

Read the text and complete the graphic organizer.

People have the ability to either harm or help the environment. Each day, humans make choices that affect Earth in negative or positive ways.

People can affect Earth in a negative way by using increasing amounts of natural resources like freshwater or trees. Other examples of the negative impacts of people include air, water, and soil pollution, and the massive amounts of garbage and waste people produce every day.

· Resource demand – As the number of people in the world grows, a strain is put on natural resources that people need. Some resources, like <u>fossil fuels</u>, cannot be replaced.

· Pollution – Humans have been very successful in creating products and technologies to improve their lives. However, many of those products and technologies have led to pollution in the soil, water, and air from waste and byproducts.

· Waste production – The average American throws away about 4 pounds of trash per day. Think how much that is in a year—and that's just garbage generated in the United States!

You may be thinking, "These are such big problems to solve!" You may believe there is nothing you can do to help save and improve the environment. But every day, people can make choices that affect Earth in positive ways. Examples include:

· Plant trees – Trees release oxygen and help provide homes and resources for animals.

· Drive less – Ride a bike, walk, or carpool as a way to cut down on air pollution and use less fuel.

· Save water – Don't waste water! Take shorter showers, and don't leave the faucet running.

· Save energy – Turn off any electronics or lights when they are not in use.

- Recycle and Reuse – Recycle bottles, cans, and boxes instead of just throwing them away. Buy products that can be reused in a different way.
- Buy <u>biodegradable</u> products that will break down easily in the environment.

PART A: Use the text to identify each statement as **true** or **false**.

1. _____ People only have a negative effect on Earth's environment.

2. _____ Some natural resources cannot be replaced.

3. _____ The growing world population has no effect on the use of natural resources.

4. _____ Planting trees is a way to help replace a natural resource.

5. _____ Riding a bike or walking instead of riding in a car are ways to cut down on air pollution.

PART B: Use the text to answer the questions.

6. A. Use a dictionary to define <u>fossil fuels</u>.
   B. Why are fossil fuels so important? What are they used to create?

7. Use the text to infer the definition of <u>biodegradable</u>. Use a dictionary to see if your definition is correct.

8. List 6 ways people can affect Earth positively. Which ones can you do?

PART C: Writing and research prompts

9. British author Thomas Fuller said, "We never know the worth of water until the well is dry." Write the meaning of the quote in your own words.

10. Do you think you throw away 4 pounds of trash per day? Track your family's waste production for a week. Make a chart with your results.

11. Divide into groups. Research additional ways that people can conserve resources and help improve the environment. Present your ideas to the class and discuss.

Problem-Solution-Results

Choose an environmental problem like air pollution or waste disposal. Use classroom or online resources to research the problem and complete the graphic organizer.

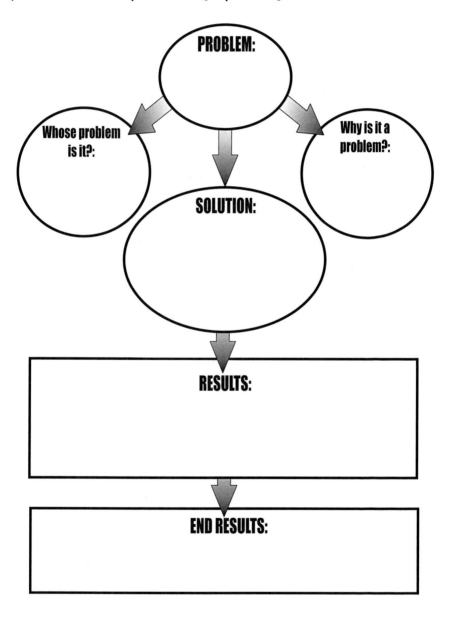

PROBLEM:

Whose problem is it?:

Why is it a problem?:

SOLUTION:

RESULTS:

END RESULTS:

PRIMARY SOURCE ANALYSIS

Water Pollution

Coal is an energy source buried deep underground. It is primarily used to generate electricity for homes and businesses. Coal mining is an important industry that provides many jobs. Coal plants use technology to reduce pollution but still produce waste that can lead to <u>contaminated</u> air and water.

Analyze the picture and answer the questions.

Courtesy of National Archives and Records Administration

Woman holds undrinkable water from her well near eastern Ohio coal mines (1973)

1. Use a dictionary to define <u>contaminated</u>. List a synonym and an antonym.

2. What is the setting of this photograph (home or business)?

3. Use the text to infer what the substance is in the jar.

4. Infer the woman's emotions from the text, her facial expression, and the jar she is holding.

5. Predict what actions the woman will take about the contaminated water in her well.

6. Coal provides 44% of the energy in the U.S. Weigh the benefits of coal-produced energy against the costs of pollution. Write your opinion in a well-developed paragraph. Discuss as a class.

What Is the EPA?

Read the text and answer the questions.

My teacher gave our class an assignment today. We had to write a report about the EPA and what it does. I didn't know what EPA stood for until I looked it up! EPA stands for Environmental Protection <u>Agency</u>. It is an agency set up by the government to write and enforce rules that help protect the environment. President Nixon set up the EPA in 1970. It has made a big impact on cleaning up the environment in the United States!

One of my favorite things to do is to go to the lake. I love fishing, swimming, and just being outside. Did you know there was a time when people were afraid to swim in some lakes because they were so badly polluted? Decades ago, many lakes and rivers were filled with trash, oil, and toxic waste. Fish even died in the poisonous water. Air pollution from factories and cars was a real problem, too. In some big cities, the air was dangerous for people to breathe.

It took many years for changes to occur, but the EPA helped pass laws that made lakes, rivers, and ocean water cleaner and safer. Businesses were not allowed to dump their waste products into the water anymore. The EPA worked to reduce dangerous pollutants in the air. It also helped pass laws to reduce the number of toxic chemicals used in household items.

The EPA has helped make Earth a healthier and cleaner place to live!

1. Use a dictionary to define <u>agency</u> as it is used in the text.

2. A. What does EPA stand for?
   B. Summarize the purpose of the EPA.

3. What was the environment's condition before the EPA was formed?

4. Predict what might have happened if a government agency like the EPA had not been formed.

5. Each state has its own environmental agency. Research your state's agency. Write a summary of important environmental issues in your state, and what the agency is doing to solve them.

The Price of Success

Look at the image and answer the questions.

Spoils of **Success**

Courtesy of Bigstock.com

1. Use a dictionary to define <u>spoils</u> and <u>success</u> as they are used in the caption.

2. A. What do you see in the background? Does it represent spoils or success?
   B. What do you see in the foreground? Does it represent spoils or success?

3. Explain the relationship between the city and the pollution/trash.

4. Is the city's success worth the harm caused to the environment? Defend your opinion.

5. Create your own cartoon to illustrate a solution to the problem presented in the above cartoon. Display and discuss your cartoons as a class.

The Problem of Oil Spills

Read the text and answer the questions.

Oil spills into oceans, rivers, or bays can cause great damage to the environment. Oil spills are most often caused by accidents. These accidents may involve tankers that carry the oil or equipment used to transport oil or drill for it. Sometimes a natural disaster like a hurricane can cause an oil spill.

Most oil spills are caused by people, whether their actions are accidental or <u>deliberate</u>. One example of a deliberate act is someone illegally dumping crude oil into the ocean to avoid the cost of disposing of it properly. Another example is when a country dumps oil into another country's water in an act of terrorism.

Water and oil do not mix. Because of this, spilled oil sits on the water's surface and can be very harmful to birds, animals, fish, and other marine life. Animals and birds often become coated with oil. This can lead to their deaths if the oil is not cleaned off. The entire food chain in an area can be affected when tiny marine creatures like plankton die from an oil spill.

There are many ways to clean up an oil spill. The method chosen depends on the circumstances of the spill. Unfortunately, some methods can cause more problems. Chemicals can be used to break up the oil, but they may further pollute the environment. If the oil spill is very large, the oil can be burned. However, this leads to air pollution. Other methods include skimmers that scoop up the oil and "sorbents," big sponges that absorb oil.

1. Use a dictionary to define <u>deliberate</u> as it is used in the text.

2. Complete the graphic organizer to list causes and effects of oil spills.

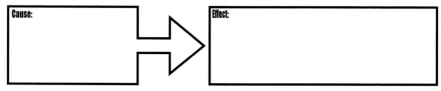

Cause: Effect:

3. Why doesn't oil just sink to the bottom of a body of water when it spills? How does this threaten marine life?

4. List the advantages and disadvantages of various methods to clean up an oil spill. Cite evidence from the text.

Cleaning Up Oil Spills

Conduct the following experiment and answer the questions.

Purpose:

To reproduce the effects of an oil spill, and apply an effective way to clean it up

Materials Needed:

aluminum foil • vegetable oil • deep baking dish • water • cotton balls

Experiment Time:

Approximately 15 minutes

Procedure:

1. Pour water into the dish until it is half full.
2. Shape aluminum foil into a small boat about 2 inches long.
3. Fill the boat with cooking oil and place it in the dish on top of the water.
4. Tip the boat over to create an "oil spill."
5. Observe as the oil contaminates the water and begins to spread.
6. Clean up the oil spill. Use cotton balls to soak up the oil by placing them over the contaminated areas.

---

1. Take note of how many cotton balls you need to clean up the "oil spill." Imagine millions of gallons of oil being spilled into the ocean. Discuss the amount of effort needed to clean up that oil spill.

2. Observe how the oil spreads across the water. If the water were rough or had waves, would the oil spread faster or slower? Keeping this in mind, do you think it would be hardest to clean up an oil spill in an ocean, lake, or river?

3. Which cleanup method did you simulate with the cotton? Explain your answer.
   A. skimming   B. sorbent   C. chemical dispersant

4. Summarize the experiment and your results in a well-organized paragraph.

Correlations to Common Core State Standards

For your convenience, correlations are listed page-by-page and for the entire book!

This book is correlated to the Common Core State Standards for English Language Arts grades 3-8, and to Common Core State Standards for Literacy in History, Science, & Technological Subjects grades 6-8.

Correlations are highlighted in gray.

PAGE #	READING — Includes: RI: Reading Informational Text / RH: Reading History	WRITING — Includes: W: Writing / WHST: Writing History, Science, & Technology	LANGUAGE — Includes: L: Language / LF: Language Foundational Skills	SPEAKING & LISTENING — Includes: SL: Speaking & Listening
2	RI 1 2 3 4 5 6 7 8 9 10 / RH	W 1 2 3 4 5 6 7 8 9 10 / WHST	L 1 2 3 4 5 6 / LF	SL 1 2 3 4 5 6
3	RI 1 2 3 4 5 6 7 8 9 10 / RH	W 1 2 3 4 5 6 7 8 9 10 / WHST	L 1 2 3 4 5 6 / LF	SL 1 2 3 4 5 6
4	RI 1 2 3 4 5 6 7 8 9 10 / RH	W 1 2 3 4 5 6 7 8 9 10 / WHST	L 1 2 3 4 5 6 / LF	SL 1 2 3 4 5 6
5	RI 1 2 3 4 5 6 7 8 9 10 / RH	W 1 2 3 4 5 6 7 8 9 10 / WHST	L 1 2 3 4 5 6 / LF	SL 1 2 3 4 5 6
6	RI 1 2 3 4 5 6 7 8 9 10 / RH	W 1 2 3 4 5 6 7 8 9 10 / WHST	L 1 2 3 4 5 6 / LF	SL 1 2 3 4 5 6
7	RI 1 2 3 4 5 6 7 8 9 10 / RH	W 1 2 3 4 5 6 7 8 9 10 / WHST	L 1 2 3 4 5 6 / LF	SL 1 2 3 4 5 6
8	RI 1 2 3 4 5 6 7 8 9 10 / RH	W 1 2 3 4 5 6 7 8 9 10 / WHST	L 1 2 3 4 5 6 / LF	SL 1 2 3 4 5 6
9	RI 1 2 3 4 5 6 7 8 9 10 / RH	W 1 2 3 4 5 6 7 8 9 10 / WHST	L 1 2 3 4 5 6 / LF	SL 1 2 3 4 5 6
10-11	RI 1 2 3 4 5 6 7 8 9 10 / RH	W 1 2 3 4 5 6 7 8 9 10 / WHST	L 1 2 3 4 5 6 / LF	SL 1 2 3 4 5 6
12-13	RI 1 2 3 4 5 6 7 8 9 10 / RH	W 1 2 3 4 5 6 7 8 9 10 / WHST	L 1 2 3 4 5 6 / LF	SL 1 2 3 4 5 6
14	RI 1 2 3 4 5 6 7 8 9 10 / RH	W 1 2 3 4 5 6 7 8 9 10 / WHST	L 1 2 3 4 5 6 / LF	SL 1 2 3 4 5 6
15	RI 1 2 3 4 5 6 7 8 9 10 / RH	W 1 2 3 4 5 6 7 8 9 10 / WHST	L 1 2 3 4 5 6 / LF	SL 1 2 3 4 5 6
16-17	RI 1 2 3 4 5 6 7 8 9 10 / RH	W 1 2 3 4 5 6 7 8 9 10 / WHST	L 1 2 3 4 5 6 / LF	SL 1 2 3 4 5 6
18	RI 1 2 3 4 5 6 7 8 9 10 / RH	W 1 2 3 4 5 6 7 8 9 10 / WHST	L 1 2 3 4 5 6 / LF	SL 1 2 3 4 5 6
19	RI 1 2 3 4 5 6 7 8 9 10 / RH	W 1 2 3 4 5 6 7 8 9 10 / WHST	L 1 2 3 4 5 6 / LF	SL 1 2 3 4 5 6
20	RI 1 2 3 4 5 6 7 8 9 10 / RH	W 1 2 3 4 5 6 7 8 9 10 / WHST	L 1 2 3 4 5 6 / LF	SL 1 2 3 4 5 6
21	RI 1 2 3 4 5 6 7 8 9 10 / RH	W 1 2 3 4 5 6 7 8 9 10 / WHST	L 1 2 3 4 5 6 / LF	SL 1 2 3 4 5 6
22	RI 1 2 3 4 5 6 7 8 9 10 / RH	W 1 2 3 4 5 6 7 8 9 10 / WHST	L 1 2 3 4 5 6 / LF	SL 1 2 3 4 5 6
23	RI 1 2 3 4 5 6 7 8 9 10 / RH	W 1 2 3 4 5 6 7 8 9 10 / WHST	L 1 2 3 4 5 6 / LF	SL 1 2 3 4 5 6
COMPLETE BOOK	RI 1 2 3 4 5 6 7 8 9 10 / RH	W 1 2 3 4 5 6 7 8 9 10 / WHST	L 1 2 3 4 5 6 / LF	SL 1 2 3 4 5 6

For the complete Common Core standard identifier, combine your grade + "." + letter code above + "." + number code above.

In addition to the correlations indicated here, the activities may be adapted or expanded to align to additional standards and to meet the diverse needs of your unique students!